A Crochet Jo

A Journal for Crochet P

A Crochet Journal to help keep your patterns, projects, yarn and supplies organized

By Craftdrawer Craft Patterns

www.craftdrawer.com

© Copyright 2016 All Rights Reserved

Table of Contents

What's Inside

Crochet References

Crochet Hook Sizes

Crochet Project Journal*

A Place for Notes*

Project Planner*

Project Calendar*

Measurements*

Yarn Inventory*

Shopping List for Yarn and Supplies*

Additional Projects Ideas Notes

Note - There are 12 pages each in order for you to track at least one year of projects

A Crochet Journal

The Crochet Journal is a way to keep your projects, patterns, yarn, and ideas organized. If you are looking for a way to track your pattern notes, yarn inventory, supplies that you need for a projects, this journal will help you keep them all together in one easy spot.

The journal includes pages to track the progress of your current project, a planner for ideas and upcoming projects, a list for your yarn inventory, a supply list to write down what you need for a new ideas and much more.

There are enough pages for at least one years worth of projects in all. Plus there is even a page to track measurements for those who crochet clothing items.

Whether your next crochet project is an afghan, hat, scarf or sweater the Crochet Journal will be a helpful tool to keep track of your progress, make sure you stock enough yarn for your next idea and more.

We hope you enjoy the journal and leave us positive feedback or suggestions on any positive changes we can make on this publication to help you on your crochet journey.

Visit us online at
www.craftddrawer.com

© Copyright 2016 Craftdrawer Crafts all right reserved - Do not distribute or reprint this journal book without the permission of the author.

Crochet References

A Quick Guide for Crochet Terms and Crochet Slang

Crochet Abbreviation Guide

alt = alternate approx = approximately beg = begin(ning) bet = between BL/bk lp = back loop(s) BLO = back loop only bo = bobble BP = back post BPdc = back post double crochet(s) BPsc = back post single crochet(s) BPtr = back post triple crochet(s) CA = color A CB = color B CC = contrasting color ch(s) = chain(s) ch- = refers to chain previously made/worked ch-sp = chain space CL(s) =cluster(s) cm = centimeter cont = continue dc = double crochet dc2tog = double crochet 2 stitches together dec = decrease dtr/d trc = double triple/treble crochet ea = each est = established	FLO = front loop only foll = follow FP = front post FPdc = front post double crochet(s) FPsc = front post single crochet(s) FPtr/FPtrc = front post triple/treble crochet(s) FL/ft lp = front loop(s) g = gram grp(s) = groups hdc = half double crochet hk = hook inc = increase lp(s) = loop(s) lp st = loop stitch MC = main color m = meters mm = millimeters O = yarn over oz = ounce(s) p = picot pat(s) = pattern(s) PC(s) = popcorn(s) pm = place maker prev = previous *Continued on next page....*

Crochet Abbreviations Continued

rem = remain rep = repeat(s) rev sc/reverse sc = reverse single crochet rnd(s) = round(s) RS = right side sc = single crochet sc2tog = single crochet 2 stitches together sdc = short double crochet sk = skip(ped) sl st = slip stitch sp(s) = space(s) st(s) = stitch(es)	tch/t-ch = turning chain tog = together tr/trc = treble/triple crochet tr tr/tr trc = triple treble crochet/triple triple crochet WS = wrong side X-st = cross-stitch yd = yard(s) yo = yarn over yoh = yarn over hook

Crochet Slang Terms

C2C - Corner to Corner
CAL - Crochet Along
FOTH - Fresh off the Hook
Frogging - Ripping out or undoing rows or rounds of crochet (ribbit)
HOTH - Hot off the Hook
Stash - Special Treasures all Secretly Hidden
WIP - Work in Progress
UFO - Unfinished Projects
Yarn Bomb - A decorative object of crochet or knitted art placed in a public area

Crochet Symbols

The Crochet Yarn Council has a FREE PDF file with Crochet symbols that you can download and print. You can find it here on their website -

Free Printable Crochet Symbols Chart

Knitting Needles and Crochet Hook Sizes

Metric diameter	Knitting needle diameter	Crochet hook size
2.25 mm	1	B-1
2.75 mm	2	C-2
3.25 mm	3	D-3
3.5 mm	4	E-4
3.75 mm	5	F-5
4 mm	6	G-6
4.5 mm	7	7
5 mm	8	H-8
5.5 mm	9	I-9
6 mm	10	J-10
6.5 mm	10.5	K-10.5
8 mm	11	L-11
9 mm	13	M/N-13
10 mm	15	N/P-15
12.75 mm	17	—
15 mm	19	P/Q
16 mm	—	Q
19 mm	35	S
25 mm	50	—

Crochet Project Journal

Project Description:_____

Date Started:_____

Completion Date:_____

Gift Recipient:_____

Pattern Information

Pattern Name:_____

Designer/Publisher:_____

Source:_____

Yarn Information

Yarn Brand/Type:_____

Color/ Dye Lot:_____

Fiber Content:_____

Yarn Weight/Yardage:_____

No. Skeins/Yardage:_____

Yarn Purchased From:_____

Project Information

Size:_____

Hook Size(s):_____

Gauge:_____

Special
Instructions:_____

Insert Project Photo Here

Tape Yarn Sample Here

Crochet Project Notes

Project Planner

Project Name	Description Start Date

Crochet Calendar

Month			Year			
Sunday	Monday	Tuesday	Wednesday	Thursday	Friday	Saturday

Measurements

Shoulders

Shoulder length/left:_____ right:_____

Shoulder-to-shoulder/front:_____

Shoulder-to-shoulder/back:_____

Back width:_____

Front shoulder slope/left:_____ right:_____

Back shoulder slope/left:_____ right:_____

Neck to waist/front:_____

Neck to waist/back:_____

Arms

Arm length (over arm)/left:_____ right:_____

Biceps/upper arm circumference/left:_____ right:_____

Armhole depth/left:_____ right:_____

Bust

Bust circumference:_____

Upper bust circumference:_____

Under bust circumference:_____

Chest width:_____

Photo: Notes:

Neck

Natural neckline:_____

Neck edge to bust point
 (bust depth)/left:_____ right:_____

Neck edge to waist/left:_____ right:_____

Legs

Outer seam/left:_____ right:_____

Inseam:_____

Waist to floor/front:_____

Waist to floor/back:_____

Crotch

Crotch length/total:_____

Crotch length/front:_____

Crotch length/back:_____

Waist to floor/front:_____

Waist to floor/back:_____

Crotch

Crotch length/total:_____

Crotch length/front:_____

Crotch length/back:_____

Crotch depth:_____

Waist and hips

Waist circumference:_____

Abdomen:_____

Abdomen depth:_____

Hip circumference:_____

Hip depth:_____

Fullest part of hip:_____

Fullest hip depth:_____

Yarn Inventory

Brand: _____

Color: _____

Lot: _____

_____

Brand: _____

Color: _____

Lot: _____

_____

Brand: _____

Color: _____

Lot: _____

_____

Brand: _____

Color: _____

Lot: _____

_____

Brand: _____

Color: _____

Lot: _____

_____

_____

Crochet Supplies Project Shopping List

Yarn Needed:

_____

_____

_____

_____

_____

Crochet Hooks:

_____

_____

_____

Other Supplies and Material:

_____

_____

_____

_____

_____

Crochet Project Journal

Project Description:_____

Date Started:_____

Completion Date:_____

Gift Recipient:_____

Pattern Information

Pattern Name:_____

Designer/Publisher:_____

Source:_____

Yarn Information

Yarn Brand/Type:_____

Color/ Dye Lot:_____

Fiber Content:_____

Yarn Weight/Yardage:_____

No. Skeins/Yardage:_____

Yarn Purchased From:_____

Project Information

Size:_____

Hook Size(s):_____

Gauge:_____

Special Instructions:_____

Insert Project Photo Here

Tape Yarn Sample Here

Crochet Project Notes

Project Planner

Project Name	Description Start Date

Crochet Calendar

Month						Year
Sunday	Monday	Tuesday	Wednesday	Thursday	Friday	Saturday

Measurements

Shoulders

Shoulder length/left:_____ right:_____

Shoulder-to-shoulder/front:_____

Shoulder-to-shoulder/back:_____

Back width:_____

Front shoulder slope/left:_____ right:_____

Back shoulder slope/left:_____ right:_____

Neck to waist/front:_____

Neck to waist/back:_____

Arms

Arm length (over arm)/left:_____ right:_____

Biceps/upper arm circumference/left:_____ right:_____

Armhole depth/left:_____ right:_____

Bust

Bust circumference:_____

Upper bust circumference:_____

Under bust circumference:_____

Chest width:_____

Photo: Notes:

Neck

Natural neckline:_____

Neck edge to bust point
    (bust depth)/left:_____ right:_____

Neck edge to waist/left:_____ right:_____

Legs

Outer seam/left:_____ right:_____

Inseam:_____

Waist to floor/front:_____

Waist to floor/back:_____

Crotch

Crotch length/total:_____

Crotch length/front:_____

Crotch length/back:_____

Waist to floor/front:_____

Waist to floor/back:_____

Crotch

Crotch length/total:_____

Crotch length/front:_____

Crotch length/back:_____

Crotch depth:_____

Waist and hips

Waist circumference:_____

Abdomen:_____

Abdomen depth:_____

Hip circumference:_____

Hip depth:_____

Fullest part of hip:_____

Fullest hip depth:_____

Yarn Inventory

Brand: _____

Color: _____

Lot: _____

_____

Brand: _____

Color: _____

Lot: _____

_____

Brand: _____

Color: _____

Lot: _____

_____

Brand: _____

Color: _____

Lot: _____

_____

Brand: _____

Color: _____

Lot: _____

_____

Crochet Supplies Project Shopping List

Yarn Needed:

_____

_____

_____

_____

_____

Crochet Hooks:

_____

_____

_____

Other Supplies and Material:

_____

_____

_____

_____

_____

Crochet Project Journal

Project Description:_____

Date Started:_____

Completion Date:_____

Gift Recipient:_____

Pattern Information

Pattern Name:_____

Designer/Publisher:_____

Source:_____

Yarn Information

Yarn Brand/Type:_____

Color/ Dye Lot:_____

Fiber Content:_____

Yarn Weight/Yardage:_____

No. Skeins/Yardage:_____

Yarn Purchased From:_____

Project Information

Size:_____

Hook Size(s):_____

Gauge:_____

Special Instructions:_____

Insert Project Photo Here

Tape Yarn Sample Here

Crochet Project Notes

Project Planner

Project Name	Description Start Date

Crochet Calendar

Month			Year			
Sunday	Monday	Tuesday	Wednesday	Thursday	Friday	Saturday

Measurements

Shoulders

Shoulder length/left:_____ right:_____

Shoulder-to-shoulder/front:_____

Shoulder-to-shoulder/back:_____

Back width:_____

Front shoulder slope/left:_____ right:_____

Back shoulder slope/left:_____ right:_____

Neck to waist/front:_____

Neck to waist/back:_____

Arms

Arm length (over arm)/left:_____ right:_____

Biceps/upper arm circumference/left:_____ right:_____

Armhole depth/left:_____ right:_____

Bust

Bust circumference:_____

Upper bust circumference:_____

Under bust circumference:_____

Chest width:_____

Photo: Notes:

Neck

Natural neckline:_____

Neck edge to bust point
 (bust depth)/left:_____ right:_____

Neck edge to waist/left:_____ right:_____

Legs

Outer seam/left:_____ right:_____

Inseam:_____

Waist to floor/front:_____

Waist to floor/back:_____

Crotch

Crotch length/total:_____

Crotch length/front:_____

Crotch length/back:_____

Waist to floor/front:_____

Waist to floor/back:_____

Crotch

Crotch length/total:_____

Crotch length/front:_____

Crotch length/back:_____

Crotch depth:_____

Waist and hips

Waist circumference:_____

Abdomen:_____

Abdomen depth:_____

Hip circumference:_____

Hip depth:_____

Fullest part of hip:_____

Fullest hip depth:_____

Yarn Inventory

Brand: _____

Color: _____

Lot: _____

_____

Brand: _____

Color: _____

Lot: _____

_____

Brand: _____

Color: _____

Lot: _____

_____

Brand: _____

Color: _____

Lot: _____

_____

Brand: _____

Color: _____

Lot: _____

_____

_____

Crochet Supplies Project Shopping List

Yarn Needed:

_____

_____

_____

_____

_____

_____

Crochet Hooks:

_____

_____

_____

_____

Other Supplies and Material:

_____

_____

_____

_____

_____

Crochet Project Journal

Project Description:_____

Date Started:_____

Completion Date:_____

Gift Recipient:_____

Pattern Information

Pattern Name:_____

Designer/Publisher:_____

Source:_____

Yarn Information

Yarn Brand/Type:_____

Color/ Dye Lot:_____

Fiber Content:_____

Yarn Weight/Yardage:_____

No. Skeins/Yardage:_____

Yarn Purchased From:_____

Project Information

Size:_____

Hook Size(s):_____

Gauge:_____

Special Instructions:_____

Insert Project Photo Here

Tape Yarn Sample Here

Crochet Project Notes

Project Planner

Project Name	Description Start Date

Crochet Calendar

Month			Year			
Sunday	Monday	Tuesday	Wednesday	Thursday	Friday	Saturday

Measurements

Shoulders

Shoulder length/left:_____ right:_____

Shoulder-to-shoulder/front:_____

Shoulder-to-shoulder/back:_____

Back width:_____

Front shoulder slope/left:_____ right:_____

Back shoulder slope/left:_____ right:_____

Neck to waist/front:_____

Neck to waist/back:_____

Arms

Arm length (over arm)/left:_____ right:_____

Biceps/upper arm circumference/left:_____ right:_____

Armhole depth/left:_____ right:_____

Bust

Bust circumference:_____

Upper bust circumference:_____

Under bust circumference:_____

Chest width:_____

Photo: Notes:

Neck

Natural neckline:_____

Neck edge to bust point (bust depth)/left:_____ right:_____

Neck edge to waist/left:_____ right:_____

Legs

Outer seam/left:_____ right:_____

Inseam:_____

Waist to floor/front:_____

Waist to floor/back:_____

Crotch

Crotch length/total:_____

Crotch length/front:_____

Crotch length/back:_____

Waist to floor/front:_____

Waist to floor/back:_____

Crotch

Crotch length/total:_____

Crotch length/front:_____

Crotch length/back:_____

Crotch depth:_____

Waist and hips

Waist circumference:_____

Abdomen:_____

Abdomen depth:_____

Hip circumference:_____

Hip depth:_____

Fullest part of hip:_____

Fullest hip depth:_____

Yarn Inventory

Brand: _____

Color: _____

Lot: _____

_____

Brand: _____

Color: _____

Lot: _____

_____

Brand: _____

Color: _____

Lot: _____

_____

Brand: _____

Color: _____

Lot: _____

_____

Brand: _____

Color: _____

Lot: _____

_____

_____

Crochet Supplies Project Shopping List

Yarn Needed:

_____

_____

_____

_____

_____

Crochet Hooks:

_____

_____

_____

Other Supplies and Material:

_____

_____

_____

_____

_____

Crochet Project Journal

Project Description:_____

Date Started:_____

Completion Date:_____

Gift Recipient:_____

Pattern Information

Pattern Name:_____

Designer/Publisher:_____

Source:_____

Yarn Information

Yarn Brand/Type:_____

Color/ Dye Lot:_____

Fiber Content:_____

Yarn Weight/Yardage:_____

No. Skeins/Yardage:_____

Yarn Purchased From:_____

Project Information

Size:_____

Hook Size(s):_____

Gauge:_____

Special
Instructions:_____

Insert Project Photo Here

Tape Yarn Sample Here

Crochet Project Notes

Project Planner

Project Name	Description Start Date

Crochet Calendar

Month						Year
Sunday	Monday	Tuesday	Wednesday	Thursday	Friday	Saturday

Measurements

Shoulders

Shoulder length/left:_____ right:_____

Shoulder-to-shoulder/front:_____

Shoulder-to-shoulder/back:_____

Back width:_____

Front shoulder slope/left:_____ right:_____

Back shoulder slope/left:_____ right:_____

Neck to waist/front:_____

Neck to waist/back:_____

Arms

Arm length (over arm)/left:_____ right:_____

Biceps/upper arm circumference/left:_____ right:_____

Armhole depth/left:_____ right:_____

Bust

Bust circumference:_____

Upper bust circumference:_____

Under bust circumference:_____

Chest width:_____

Photo: Notes:

Neck

Natural neckline:_____

Neck edge to bust point
  (bust depth)/left:_____ right:_____

Neck edge to waist/left:_____ right:_____

Legs

Outer seam/left:_____ right:_____

Inseam:_____

Waist to floor/front:_____

Waist to floor/back:_____

Crotch

Crotch length/total:_____

Crotch length/front:_____

Crotch length/back:_____

Waist to floor/front:_____

Waist to floor/back:_____

Crotch

Crotch length/total:_____

Crotch length/front:_____

Crotch length/back:_____

Crotch depth:_____

Waist and hips

Waist circumference:_____

Abdomen:_____

Abdomen depth:_____

Hip circumference:_____

Hip depth:_____

Fullest part of hip:_____

Fullest hip depth:_____

Yarn Inventory

Brand: _____

Color: _____

Lot: _____

_____

Brand: _____

Color: _____

Lot: _____

_____

Brand: _____

Color: _____

Lot: _____

_____

Brand: _____

Color: _____

Lot: _____

_____

Brand: _____

Color: _____

Lot: _____

_____

_____

Crochet Supplies Project Shopping List

Yarn Needed:

_____

_____

_____

_____

_____

_____

Crochet Hooks:

_____

_____

_____

_____

Other Supplies and Material:

_____

_____

_____

_____

_____

Crochet Project Journal

Project Description:_____

Date Started:_____

Completion Date:_____

Gift Recipient:_____

Pattern Information

Pattern Name:_____

Designer/Publisher:_____

Source:_____

Yarn Information

Yarn Brand/Type:_____

Color/ Dye Lot:_____

Fiber Content:_____

Yarn Weight/Yardage:_____

No. Skeins/Yardage:_____

Yarn Purchased From:_____

Project Information

Size:_____

Hook Size(s):_____

Gauge:_____

Special Instructions:_____

Insert Project Photo Here

Tape Yarn Sample Here

Crochet Project Notes

Project Planner

Project Name	Description Start Date

Crochet Calendar

Month			Year			
Sunday	Monday	Tuesday	Wednesday	Thursday	Friday	Saturday

Measurements

Shoulders

Shoulder length/left:_____ right:_____

Shoulder-to-shoulder/front:_____

Shoulder-to-shoulder/back:_____

Back width:_____

Front shoulder slope/left:_____ right:_____

Back shoulder slope/left:_____ right:_____

Neck to waist/front:_____

Neck to waist/back:_____

Arms

Arm length (over arm)/left:_____ right:_____

Biceps/upper arm circumference/left:_____ right:_____

Armhole depth/left:_____ right:_____

Bust

Bust circumference:_____

Upper bust circumference:_____

Under bust circumference:_____

Chest width:_____

Photo: Notes:

Neck

Natural neckline:_____

Neck edge to bust point (bust depth)/left:_____ right:_____

Neck edge to waist/left:_____ right:_____

Legs

Outer seam/left:_____ right:_____

Inseam:_____

Waist to floor/front:_____

Waist to floor/back:_____

Crotch

Crotch length/total:_____

Crotch length/front:_____

Crotch length/back:_____

Waist to floor/front:_____

Waist to floor/back:_____

Crotch

Crotch length/total:_____

Crotch length/front:_____

Crotch length/back:_____

Crotch depth:_____

Waist and hips

Waist circumference:_____

Abdomen:_____

Abdomen depth:_____

Hip circumference:_____

Hip depth:_____

Fullest part of hip:_____

Fullest hip depth:_____

Yarn Inventory

Brand: _____

Color: _____

Lot: _____

_____

Brand: _____

Color: _____

Lot: _____

_____

Brand: _____

Color: _____

Lot: _____

_____

Brand: _____

Color: _____

Lot: _____

_____

Brand: _____

Color: _____

Lot: _____

_____

_____

Crochet Supplies Project Shopping List

Yarn Needed:

_____

_____

_____

_____

_____

Crochet Hooks:

_____

_____

_____

Other Supplies and Material:

_____

_____

_____

_____

_____

Crochet Project Journal

Project Description:_____

Date Started:_____

Completion Date:_____

Gift Recipient:_____

Pattern Information

Pattern Name:_____

Designer/Publisher:_____

Source:_____

Yarn Information

Yarn Brand/Type:_____

Color/ Dye Lot:_____

Fiber Content:_____

Yarn Weight/Yardage:_____

No. Skeins/Yardage:_____

Yarn Purchased From:_____

Project Information

Size:_____

Hook Size(s):_____

Gauge:_____

Special Instructions:_____

Insert Project Photo Here

Tape Yarn Sample Here

Crochet Project Notes

Project Planner

Project Name	Description Start Date

Crochet Calendar

Month			Year			
Sunday	Monday	Tuesday	Wednesday	Thursday	Friday	Saturday

Measurements

Shoulders

Shoulder length/left:_____ right:_____

Shoulder-to-shoulder/front:_____

Shoulder-to-shoulder/back:_____

Back width:_____

Front shoulder slope/left:_____ right:_____

Back shoulder slope/left:_____ right:_____

Neck to waist/front:_____

Neck to waist/back:_____

Arms

Arm length (over arm)/left:_____ right:_____

Biceps/upper arm circumference/left:_____ right:_____

Armhole depth/left:_____ right:_____

Bust

Bust circumference:_____

Upper bust circumference:_____

Under bust circumference:_____

Chest width:_____

Photo: Notes:

Neck

Natural neckline:_____

Neck edge to bust point
 (bust depth)/left:_____ right:_____

Neck edge to waist/left:_____ right:_____

Legs

Outer seam/left:_____ right:_____

Inseam:_____

Waist to floor/front:_____

Waist to floor/back:_____

Crotch

Crotch length/total:_____

Crotch length/front:_____

Crotch length/back:_____

Waist to floor/front:_____

Waist to floor/back:_____

Crotch

Crotch length/total:_____

Crotch length/front:_____

Crotch length/back:_____

Crotch depth:_____

Waist and hips

Waist circumference:_____

Abdomen:_____

Abdomen depth:_____

Hip circumference:_____

Hip depth:_____

Fullest part of hip:_____

Fullest hip depth:_____

Yarn Inventory

Brand: _____

Color: _____

Lot: _____

_____

Brand: _____

Color: _____

Lot: _____

_____

Brand: _____

Color: _____

Lot: _____

_____

Brand: _____

Color: _____

Lot: _____

_____

Brand: _____

Color: _____

Lot: _____

_____

_____

Crochet Supplies Project Shopping List

Yarn Needed:

_____

_____

_____

_____

_____

_____

Crochet Hooks:

_____

_____

_____

_____

Other Supplies and Material:

_____

_____

_____

_____

_____

_____

Crochet Project Journal

Project Description:_____

Date Started:_____

Completion Date:_____

Gift Recipient:_____

Pattern Information

Pattern Name:_____

Designer/Publisher:_____

Source:_____

Yarn Information

Yarn Brand/Type:_____

Color/ Dye Lot:_____

Fiber Content:_____

Yarn Weight/Yardage:_____

No. Skeins/Yardage:_____

Yarn Purchased From:_____

Project Information

Size:_____

Hook Size(s):_____

Gauge:_____

Special Instructions:_____

Insert Project Photo Here

Tape Yarn Sample Here

Crochet Project Notes

Project Planner

Project Name	Description Start Date

Crochet Calendar

Month			Year			
Sunday	Monday	Tuesday	Wednesday	Thursday	Friday	Saturday

Measurements

Shoulders

Shoulder length/left:_____ right:_____

Shoulder-to-shoulder/front:_____

Shoulder-to-shoulder/back:_____

Back width:_____

Front shoulder slope/left:_____ right:_____

Back shoulder slope/left:_____ right:_____

Neck to waist/front:_____

Neck to waist/back:_____

Arms

Arm length (over arm)/left:_____ right:_____

Biceps/upper arm circumference/left:_____ right:_____

Armhole depth/left:_____ right:_____

Bust

Bust circumference:_____

Upper bust circumference:_____

Under bust circumference:_____

Chest width:_____

Photo: Notes:

Neck

Natural neckline:_____

Neck edge to bust point
 (bust depth)/left:_____ right:_____

Neck edge to waist/left:_____ right:_____

Legs

Outer seam/left:_____ right:_____

Inseam:_____

Waist to floor/front:_____

Waist to floor/back:_____

Crotch

Crotch length/total:_____

Crotch length/front:_____

Crotch length/back:_____

Waist to floor/front:_____

Waist to floor/back:_____

Crotch

Crotch length/total:_____

Crotch length/front:_____

Crotch length/back:_____

Crotch depth:_____

Waist and hips

Waist circumference:_____

Abdomen:_____

Abdomen depth:_____

Hip circumference:_____

Hip depth:_____

Fullest part of hip:_____

Fullest hip depth:_____

Yarn Inventory

Brand: _____

Color: _____

Lot: _____

_____

Brand: _____

Color: _____

Lot: _____

_____

Brand: _____

Color: _____

Lot: _____

_____

Brand: _____

Color: _____

Lot: _____

_____

Brand: _____

Color: _____

Lot: _____

_____

_____

Crochet Supplies Project Shopping List

Yarn Needed:

_____

_____

_____

_____

_____

Crochet Hooks:

_____

_____

_____

Other Supplies and Material:

_____

_____

_____

_____

_____

Crochet Project Journal

Project Description:_____

Date Started:_____

Completion Date:_____

Gift Recipient:_____

Pattern Information

Pattern Name:_____

Designer/Publisher:_____

Source:_____

Yarn Information

Yarn Brand/Type:_____

Color/ Dye Lot:_____

Fiber Content:_____

Yarn Weight/Yardage:_____

No. Skeins/Yardage:_____

Yarn Purchased From:_____

Project Information

Size:_____

Hook Size(s):_____

Gauge:_____

Special Instructions:_____

Insert Project Photo Here

Tape Yarn Sample Here

Crochet Project Notes

Project Planner

Project Name	Description Start Date

Crochet Calendar

Month			Year			
Sunday	Monday	Tuesday	Wednesday	Thursday	Friday	Saturday

Measurements

Shoulders

Shoulder length/left:_____ right:_____

Shoulder-to-shoulder/front:_____

Shoulder-to-shoulder/back:_____

Back width:_____

Front shoulder slope/left:_____ right:_____

Back shoulder slope/left:_____ right:_____

Neck to waist/front:_____

Neck to waist/back:_____

Arms

Arm length (over arm)/left:_____ right:_____

Biceps/upper arm circumference/left:_____ right:_____

Armhole depth/left:_____ right:_____

Bust

Bust circumference:_____

Upper bust circumference:_____

Under bust circumference:_____

Chest width:_____

Photo: Notes:

Neck

Natural neckline:_____

Neck edge to bust point
    (bust depth)/left:_____ right:_____

Neck edge to waist/left:_____ right:_____

Legs

Outer seam/left:_____ right:_____

Inseam:_____

Waist to floor/front:_____

Waist to floor/back:_____

Crotch

Crotch length/total:_____

Crotch length/front:_____

Crotch length/back:_____

Waist to floor/front:_____

Waist to floor/back:_____

Crotch

Crotch length/total:_____

Crotch length/front:_____

Crotch length/back:_____

Crotch depth:_____

Waist and hips

Waist circumference:_____

Abdomen:_____

Abdomen depth:_____

Hip circumference:_____

Hip depth:_____

Fullest part of hip:_____

Fullest hip depth:_____

Yarn Inventory

Brand: _____

Color: _____

Lot: _____

_____

Brand: _____

Color: _____

Lot: _____

_____

Brand: _____

Color: _____

Lot: _____

_____

Brand: _____

Color: _____

Lot: _____

_____

Brand: _____

Color: _____

Lot: _____

_____

_____

Crochet Supplies Project Shopping List

Yarn Needed:

_____

_____

_____

_____

_____

Crochet Hooks:

_____

_____

_____

Other Supplies and Material:

_____

_____

_____

_____

_____

Crochet Project Journal

Project Description:_____

Date Started:_____

Completion Date:_____

Gift Recipient:_____

Pattern Information

Pattern Name:_____

Designer/Publisher:_____

Source:_____

Yarn Information

Yarn Brand/Type:_____

Color/ Dye Lot:_____

Fiber Content:_____

Yarn Weight/Yardage:_____

No. Skeins/Yardage:_____

Yarn Purchased From:_____

Project Information

Size:_____

Hook Size(s):_____

Gauge:_____

Special Instructions:_____

Insert Project Photo Here

Tape Yarn Sample Here

Crochet Project Notes

Project Planner

Project Name	Description Start Date

Crochet Calendar

Month			Year			
Sunday	Monday	Tuesday	Wednesday	Thursday	Friday	Saturday

Measurements

Shoulders

Shoulder length/left:_____ right:_____

Shoulder-to-shoulder/front:_____

Shoulder-to-shoulder/back:_____

Back width:_____

Front shoulder slope/left:_____ right:_____

Back shoulder slope/left:_____ right:_____

Neck to waist/front:_____

Neck to waist/back:_____

Arms

Arm length (over arm)/left:_____ right:_____

Biceps/upper arm circumference/left:_____ right:_____

Armhole depth/left:_____ right:_____

Bust

Bust circumference:_____

Upper bust circumference:_____

Under bust circumference:_____

Chest width:_____

Photo: Notes:

Neck

Natural neckline:_____

Neck edge to bust point (bust depth)/left:_____ right:_____

Neck edge to waist/left:_____ right:_____

Legs

Outer seam/left:_____ right:_____

Inseam:_____

Waist to floor/front:_____

Waist to floor/back:_____

Crotch

Crotch length/total:_____

Crotch length/front:_____

Crotch length/back:_____

Waist to floor/front:_____

Waist to floor/back:_____

Crotch

Crotch length/total:_____

Crotch length/front:_____

Crotch length/back:_____

Crotch depth:_____

Waist and hips

Waist circumference:_____

Abdomen:_____

Abdomen depth:_____

Hip circumference:_____

Hip depth:_____

Fullest part of hip:_____

Fullest hip depth:_____

Yarn Inventory

Brand: _____

Color: _____

Lot: _____

_____

Brand: _____

Color: _____

Lot: _____

_____

Brand: _____

Color: _____

Lot: _____

_____

Brand: _____

Color: _____

Lot: _____

_____

Brand: _____

Color: _____

Lot: _____

_____

_____

Crochet Supplies Project Shopping List

Yarn Needed:

_____

_____

_____

_____

_____

Crochet Hooks:

_____

_____

_____

_____

Other Supplies and Material:

_____

_____

_____

_____

_____

_____

Crochet Project Journal

Project Description:_____

Date Started:_____

Completion Date:_____

Gift Recipient:_____

Pattern Information

Pattern Name:_____

Designer/Publisher:_____

Source:_____

Yarn Information

Yarn Brand/Type:_____

Color/ Dye Lot:_____

Fiber Content:_____

Yarn Weight/Yardage:_____

No. Skeins/Yardage:_____

Yarn Purchased From:_____

Project Information

Size:_____

Hook Size(s):_____

Gauge:_____

Special Instructions:_____

Insert Project Photo Here

Tape Yarn Sample Here

Crochet Project Notes

Project Planner

Project Name	Description Start Date

Crochet Calendar

Month			Year			
Sunday	Monday	Tuesday	Wednesday	Thursday	Friday	Saturday

Measurements

Shoulders

Shoulder length/left:_____ right:_____

Shoulder-to-shoulder/front:_____

Shoulder-to-shoulder/back:_____

Back width:_____

Front shoulder slope/left:_____ right:_____

Back shoulder slope/left:_____ right:_____

Neck to waist/front:_____

Neck to waist/back:_____

Arms

Arm length (over arm)/left:_____ right:_____

Biceps/upper arm circumference/left:_____ right:_____

Armhole depth/left:_____ right:_____

Bust

Bust circumference:_____

Upper bust circumference:_____

Under bust circumference:_____

Chest width:_____

Photo: Notes:

Neck

Natural neckline:_____

Neck edge to bust point
   (bust depth)/left:_____ right:_____

Neck edge to waist/left:_____ right:_____

Legs

Outer seam/left:_____ right:_____

Inseam:_____

Waist to floor/front:_____

Waist to floor/back:_____

Crotch

Crotch length/total:_____

Crotch length/front:_____

Crotch length/back:_____

Waist to floor/front:_____

Waist to floor/back:_____

Crotch

Crotch length/total:_____

Crotch length/front:_____

Crotch length/back:_____

Crotch depth:_____

Waist and hips

Waist circumference:_____

Abdomen:_____

Abdomen depth:_____

Hip circumference:_____

Hip depth:_____

Fullest part of hip:_____

Fullest hip depth:_____

Yarn Inventory

Brand:

Color:

Lot:

Brand:

Color:

Lot:

Brand:

Color:

Lot:

Brand:

Color:

Lot:

Brand:

Color:

Lot:

Crochet Supplies Project Shopping List

Yarn Needed:

_____

_____

_____

_____

_____

Crochet Hooks:

_____

_____

_____

_____

Other Supplies and Material:

_____

_____

_____

_____

_____

_____

Crochet Project Journal

Project Description:_____

Date Started:_____

Completion Date:_____

Gift Recipient:_____

Pattern Information

Pattern Name:_____

Designer/Publisher:_____

Source:_____

Yarn Information

Yarn Brand/Type:_____

Color/ Dye Lot:_____

Fiber Content:_____

Yarn Weight/Yardage:_____

No. Skeins/Yardage:_____

Yarn Purchased From:_____

Project Information

Size:_____

Hook Size(s):_____

Gauge:_____

Special Instructions:_____

| Insert Project Photo Here |

| Tape Yarn Sample Here |

Crochet Project Notes

Project Planner

Project Name	Description Start Date

Crochet Calendar

Month			Year			
Sunday	Monday	Tuesday	Wednesday	Thursday	Friday	Saturday

Measurements

Shoulders

Shoulder length/left:_____ right:_____

Shoulder-to-shoulder/front:_____

Shoulder-to-shoulder/back:_____

Back width:_____

Front shoulder slope/left:_____ right:_____

Back shoulder slope/left:_____ right:_____

Neck to waist/front:_____

Neck to waist/back:_____

Arms

Arm length (over arm)/left:_____ right:_____

Biceps/upper arm circumference/left:_____ right:_____

Armhole depth/left:_____ right:_____

Bust

Bust circumference:_____

Upper bust circumference:_____

Under bust circumference:_____

Chest width:_____

Photo: Notes:

Neck

Natural neckline:_____

Neck edge to bust point
(bust depth)/left:_____ right:_____

Neck edge to waist/left:_____ right:_____

Legs

Outer seam/left:_____ right:_____

Inseam:_____

Waist to floor/front:_____

Waist to floor/back:_____

Crotch

Crotch length/total:_____

Crotch length/front:_____

Crotch length/back:_____

Waist to floor/front:_____

Waist to floor/back:_____

Crotch

Crotch length/total:_____

Crotch length/front:_____

Crotch length/back:_____

Crotch depth:_____

Waist and hips

Waist circumference:_____

Abdomen:_____

Abdomen depth:_____

Hip circumference:_____

Hip depth:_____

Fullest part of hip:_____

Fullest hip depth:_____

Yarn Inventory

Brand: _____

Color: _____

Lot: _____

_____

Brand: _____

Color: _____

Lot: _____

_____

Brand: _____

Color: _____

Lot: _____

_____

Brand: _____

Color: _____

Lot: _____

_____

Brand: _____

Color: _____

Lot: _____

_____

_____

Crochet Supplies Project Shopping List

Yarn Needed:

_____

_____

_____

_____

_____

_____

Crochet Hooks:

_____

_____

_____

_____

Other Supplies and Material:

_____

_____

_____

_____

_____

_____

Additional Project Ideas and Notes

©Copyright 2016 Craftdrawer Crafts

Printed in Great Britain
by Amazon